CITIES OF THE WORLD

DALLAS

BY DEBORAH KENT

 CHILDREN'S PRESS®
A Division of Grolier Publishing
New York London Hong Kong Sydney
Danbury, Connecticut

CONSULTANTS

David O'Donald Cullen, Ph.D.
Professor of History, Collin County Community College, Plano, Texas

Linda Cornwell
Coordinator of School Quality and Professional Improvement
Indiana State Teachers Association

Project Editor: Downing Publishing Services
Design Director: Karen Kohn & Associates, Ltd.
Photo Researcher: Jan Izzo

Library of Congress Cataloging-in-Publication Data
Kent, Deborah
    Dallas / by Deborah Kent.
     p. cm. — (Cities of the world)
    Includes bibliographical references and index.
    Summary: Describes the history, culture, people, commerce, and points
of interest of Dallas, the second largest city in Texas.
    ISBN 0-516-21678-3 (lib. bdg.)   0-516-27168-7 (pbk.)
    1. Dallas (Tex.)—Juvenile literature. [1. Dallas (Tex.)] I. Title.
II. Series: Cities of the world (New York, N.Y.)
F394.D214K46 2000   00-024028
976.4'2812—dc21

GROLIER
PUBLISHING

TABLE OF CONTENTS

T E X A S

Anyone arriving by plane in Dallas, Texas, will most likely touch down at Dallas-Fort Worth (DFW) International Airport. DFW is the biggest airport in the United States. Nestled between the neighboring cities of Dallas and Fort Worth, the airport could almost be a city in its own right. It has a golf course, racquetball courts, and a medical clinic, as well as some sixty-five restaurants. Day and night, passengers from all over the world stream through the airport's maze of corridors and waiting rooms.

Of course, DFW Airport is only the starting point for a trip to Dallas. An hour-long ride in a bus, taxi, or limo brings passengers downtown, where they can see some of the city's most famous sights. There is the magnificent Union Station, built early in the twentieth century. Nearby is Reunion Arena, home to the Dallas Mavericks basketball team. There is the Dallas Arts District, a 60-acre (24-hectare) complex of museums and concert halls.

Those arriving downtown might decide to take an elevator to the top of the 50-story Reunion Tower. The observation deck in the tower's dome offers a stunning view of the city. The view is most spectacular at night, when the glass-and-steel buildings sparkle with a forest of lights.

The observation deck in the dome of the 50-story Reunion Tower (at left in this picture) offers a stunning view of the city of Dallas.

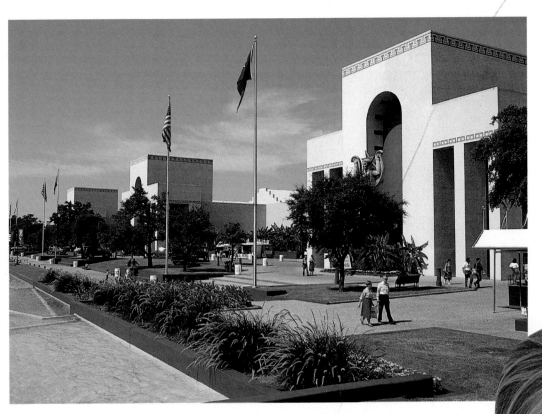

Fair Park in Dallas hosts the Texas State Fair.

A Dallas teenager wearing a plaid shirt and jeans

When Dallasites talk about their city, the word "biggest" often pops into the conversation. Dallas has the nation's biggest inland aquarium and its tallest Ferris wheel. It hosts the biggest state fair in the country and displays the largest outdoor bronze sculpture in the world. The Dallas Arts District is the biggest downtown arts and recreation complex in any U.S. city.

Visitors sometimes accuse Dallasites of boasting. But the people of Dallas have good reason to take pride in their city. Dallas is the economic and cultural center of Texas and a hub of business and culture for the south-central region of the United States. Dallas is a fascinating city to visit, and it offers a wonderful array of pleasures and opportunities to those who live there.

It has sometimes been said that Dallas is where the East peters out. With its downtown high-rise landscape and its commitment to big business, Dallas has much of the flavor of an eastern city. But it is a Texas city too, and it could also be called the gateway to the West.

WHO ARE THE DALLASITES?

About 20 percent of all
Dallasites are Hispanic.

Dallas lies on the low, rolling plains of northeastern Texas. The Trinity River divides the city into two sections, north and south. With nearby Fort Worth, Arlington, Irving, and several smaller communities, Dallas is the hub of a sprawling urban area known as the Metroplex. About 1 million people live in Dallas, making it the eighth largest city in the United States. The population of the Metroplex is 4.7 million.

Almost 50 percent of all Dallasites are people of European heritage. Some 30 percent are African Americans, and about 20 percent are Hispanics. North Dallas, the most affluent part of the city, is 80 percent white. The Highland Park neighborhood in the middle of North Dallas is among the wealthiest sections of the city. Its stately homes stand along quiet, tree-lined streets.

For generations, jobs have been scarce in South Dallas. Schools, hospitals, and other public services in this part of the city are often underfunded. Many religious, political, and business leaders are working to solve these problems. "We have a substantial degree of poverty in the midst of the plenty," a Methodist minister told reporters. "We should be doing something about it. . . . What the poor and minorities need is the same opportunity everyone else has."

A Dallas girl wearing typical garb, a cowboy hat and a white shirt

Bringing People Together

"It doesn't matter whether your ancestors came over on the Mayflower or a slave ship—we're all in the same boat now," declared Ron Kirk when he was elected mayor of Dallas in May 1995. The first African-American mayor in the city's history, Kirk won strong support from both black and white voters. In his campaign message, Kirk pledged to work toward greater racial harmony within the city. His plans to renovate downtown Dallas promised opportunities for people of all backgrounds.

THE FLESH AND THE SPIRIT

"Dallas is where you can get things," remarked a leading business executive. Ever since its founding, Dallas has been a hub of trade on the sprawling East Texas plains. Today, it is home to some of the nation's biggest shopping centers and merchandise distributors. Dallas claims more retail space per capita than any other city in the United States.

Throughout the twentieth century, Dallas has been a leader in the world of business. In 1907, Herbert Marcus opened a store that grew to become the celebrated Neiman-Marcus chain. The nation's first Seven-Eleven convenience store opened in Dallas's Oak Cliff neighborhood in 1927. In 1963, a Dallas widow named Mary Kay Ash founded a small company to sell cosmetics. Today, Mary Kay products are marketed throughout the United States and in twenty-three other countries.

Mary Kay Ash (left), the founder of Mary Kay Cosmetics, Inc., and Mary C. Crowley (right), founder of Home Interiors & Gifts, Inc. are two well-known Dallas entrepreneurs.

Herbert Marcus opened his first store in Dallas in 1907.

Below: A Dallas girl holding a bouquet of flowers

Something for Everyone

In 1959, the first Neiman-Marcus gift catalog landed in American mailboxes just in time for Christmas. The catalog specialized in luxury gift items such as gold-plated door knockers and custom-built cabinets. In honor of Dallas's western tradition, it even offered a black Angus steer. The steer could be delivered live or in steaks.

Not surprisingly, Dallas has some of the biggest shopping malls in the country. North Park Center is a mini-metropolis with palm trees, fountains, and even a skating rink. Shoppers can glory in the atmosphere while they search for discounts.

The Dallas Market Center complex is the world's largest wholesale merchandise mart, a place where retailers select and purchase products for their stores. The Market Center consists of six buildings with giant showrooms that display everything from food processors to high-heeled shoes. Dallas is one of the nation's most popular sites for conventions and trade shows. The Dallas Convention Center stands at the southern end of downtown.

Critics sometimes complain that Dallas is a city that worships the almighty dollar. But Dallas is a city of religious worship as well. With 26,000 members, the First Baptist Church of Dallas has the largest Southern Baptist congregation in the world. The church covers five blocks in downtown Dallas and sponsors twenty-two mission churches throughout the city. Dallas's First Methodist and Highland Park Methodist churches are among the ten largest Methodist churches in the country. Dallas also claims the nation's biggest Presbyterian church.

Leather western boots such as this can be found in many shops in Dallas.

A view of the Neiman-Marcus
store in North Park Center

Gold bronco pin

Though Dallas is primarily a Protestant city, it
also has several Jewish synagogues. Many Roman
Catholic churches stand in its neighborhoods as
well. One of the most revered is the Catedral
Santuario de Guadalupe (Holy Cathedral of
Guadalupe). The cathedral honors the Virgin of
Guadalupe, beloved patron of Dallas's Mexican
population.

Shoppers in a
Dallas retail store

GETTING AROUND

About one-third of the workforce in Dallas is involved in the high-tech aeronautics and defense industries. Dallas companies make airplane parts, weapons systems, and highly specialized navigation instruments for planes and rockets. Approximately one-quarter of working Dallasites have jobs in banking, insurance, and real estate. Many work in retail sales or in wholesale businesses.

Most Dallasites drive to work, fighting their way through a snarl of traffic. Until the mid-1990s, they had few other options. When a high-speed rapid-transit system was proposed for the Metroplex, many politicians and business leaders argued that it would hardly be used. They claimed Dallasites would prefer to drive, no matter how bad the traffic jams. Nevertheless, the Metroplex moved forward with plans for a high-speed light-rail system. Dallas Area Rapid Transit (DART) opened in 1996 and proved the skeptics wrong. Soon. the trains were carrying 33,000 passengers every business day—about 3,000 more than the promoters had expected. Eventually, this modern, efficient train sys-

The McKinney Avenue Trolley runs through one of Dallas's most charming shopping and dining districts.

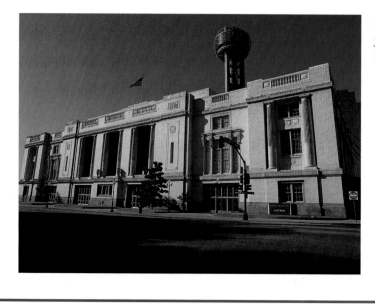

Union Station is the terminal for the remaining passenger trains that serve Dallas.

tem will have 53 miles (85 kilometers) of track and will link Dallas with many of its suburbs.

Union Station was once the hub of transportation into and out of Dallas. Opened in 1916, Union Station was like a palace to celebrate the age of steam. A magnificent staircase led to the vast second-floor waiting room, where chandeliers swung from the vaulted ceiling. The station's facade of white enameled brick is a cherished Dallas landmark. Today, much of Union Station has been converted into shops and restaurants.

But the station is still the terminal for the remaining passenger trains that serve the city.

Another relic of Dallas's past is the McKinney Avenue Trolley. Streetcars run on a 2.8-mile (4.5-km) track through one of Dallas's most charming shopping and dining districts. The trolley is a very small link in the city's transportation system, but riding it is a treat for visitors young and old.

A Dallas businessman

"We had heard a great deal about the three forks of the Trinity River and the town of Dallas. This was the center of attraction. It sounded big in far-off states. We had heard of it often. But the town—where was it? Two small log cabins, the logs just as nature formed them, chimneys made of sticks and mud, and old Mother Earth serving as floors. This was the town of Dallas, and two families, ten or twelve souls, were its population." These words are from the journal of John B. Billingsley, who arrived in Dallas in 1842.

THE TOWN ON THE TRINITY

The first people to live on the site of present-day Dallas were Native Americans who hunted game and gathered wild fruits and nuts. They did not establish permanent settlements but moved with the seasons and the herds of buffalo and other animals.

In 1841, a Tennessee lawyer named John Neely Bryan reached Texas with five companions. Bryan was not a wealthy man, but he had splendid dreams. He believed that someday the Trinity River would be a valuable route to the Gulf of Mexico. He was convinced that a settlement on the Trinity could blossom into a major trading port.

Determined to bring his dream to life, Bryan built a lean-to on a bluff overlooking the Trinity. Within a few months, his companions grew disillusioned and left. Bryan remained, with his horse and his dog for company. Eventually, other settlers joined him, including a friend from Arkansas named Joe Dallas. Some historians believe that Joe Dallas gave his name to the budding settlement.

Native Americans who hunted wild game and buffalo and gathered wild fruits and nuts were the first people to live on the site of present-day Dallas.

John Neely Bryan, founder of Dallas, and his wife

Others contend that the settlement was named after George M. Dallas, who served as U.S. vice president under James K. Polk from 1845 to 1849.

Bryan was wrong about the Trinity River. It was much too shallow for heavily laden cargo boats. Nonetheless, Bryan and the other settlers stayed on. Bryan replaced his lean-to with a sturdy log cabin, and the settlement continued to grow.

Reunion Refugees

In 1855, a band of French artists, musicians, writers, and scientists tried to establish a community outside Dallas. They hoped their village, La Reunion, would be free from poverty and strife. Within a few months, however, La Reunion failed to live up to these ideals. Disappointed, its members scattered. Most resettled in Dallas, bringing their skills and talents to the growing town. Dallasites have named many city landmarks in honor of these early settlers, including Reunion Tower, Reunion Arena, and the downtown Reunion District.

La Reunion House was built in 1855.

Present-day Texas began as the northernmost territory of Mexico. Very few Mexicans had settled in the region, which was several months' journey from their capital, Mexico City. Instead, settlers streamed in from Arkansas, Louisiana, and other parts of the United States during the 1820s and 1830s. These people, generally of northern European descent, were known to the Mexicans as Anglos.

In 1836, Texas's Anglo settlers declared their independence from Mexico and founded their own small nation. It was called the Republic of Texas, sometimes referred to as the Lone Star Republic because its flag bore a single star. Dallas was part of the Republic of Texas when John Neely Bryan settled there in

Texas celebrated its independence and became a "Free, Sovereign, and Independent Republic" on March 2, 1836.

1841. To encourage further settlement, the Republic of Texas gave Bryan a large tract of land. Bryan sold off sections of this land grant to new settlers.

Texas did not remain independent for long. Between 1846 and 1848, the United States and Mexico fought a bitter war. When the war ended, a treaty ceded a vast swath of land to the United States. This territory included Texas, New Mexico, Arizona, and parts of Utah and California. Dallas now lay within the Texas Territory, under the jurisdiction of the United States government.

Guns like this one, called the "Peacemaker," were used during the Texas Revolution, a war with Mexico that culminated in the establishment of the Republic of Texas in 1836.

During the 1820s and 1830s, settlers traveling in covered wagons streamed into Texas from Arkansas, Louisiana, and other parts of the United States.

COTTON, LONGHORNS, AND OIL

During the Civil War (1861–1865), Texas was among the Southern states that broke away from the Union. The Southern states tried to form a new nation, the Confederate States of America. Dallas served as an administrative center for the Confederate army for most of the war.

In the years after the war, northeastern Texas became an important cotton-producing region. Texas also supported vast herds of longhorn cattle on its

Right: A Texas belt buckle
Below: A cowboy guarding a herd of Texas longhorn cattle

A Texas railroad depot in the 1870s

grassy plains. Texans transported their cattle and cotton by rail to markets in the East. Dallas leaders persuaded two railroads to route their lines through the city. Early in the 1870s, Dallas became a key station on both the Houston and Texas Central and the Texas and Pacific railroads. The town bustled with railroad workers, cotton dealers, and cowboys in broad-brimmed hats.

Cowboys eating their midday meal at a chuck wagon

For years, Texas ranchers found pools of a greasy black substance on their land. They knew that this petroleum, or oil, burned easily and well. But no one had discovered how to put it to good use. The invention of the automobile changed all that. Suddenly, oil was in such demand that it was called "black gold." More than three-quarters of the oil reserves in the continental United States lie within 500 miles (805 km) of Dallas. In the early part of the twentieth century, Dallas zoomed to the top of the petroleum industry.

Cotton, cattle, and oil gave rise to a fourth major industry in Dallas—banking. Businesses with offices in Dallas naturally used banks in the city to handle their accounts. In 1913, Dallas was selected for one of twelve new Federal Reserve Banks, which instantly made the city a commercial center for the Southwest. Banking helped to spur related industries such as insurance and real estate.

Far left: Texas's long association with the oil industry is so much a part of its heritage that there is even a licorice candy called Texas Oil Drops.

Left: Cotton wagons on Elm Street, Dallas, in 1899

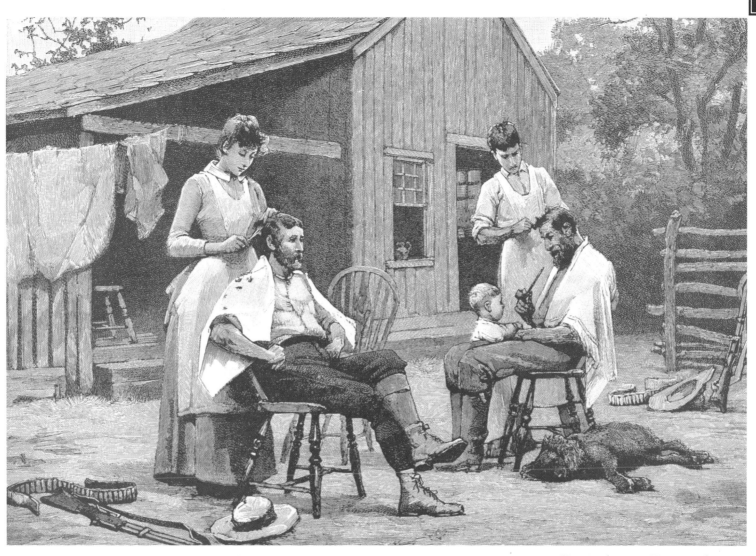

Haircut day on a Texas ranch, 1899

In sheer population, the growth of Dallas was phenomenal. In 1870, the city had fewer than 4,000 people. Twenty years later, the population had soared to 38,000, making Dallas the biggest city in Texas. Houston nudged Dallas to second place forty years later, but Dallas continued to expand.

Dallas never became the thriving river port that John Neely Bryan once envisioned. But in a sense, Bryan's dreams did come true. His settlement on the Trinity was a powerhouse of culture and trade.

TRAGEDY AND TRIUMPH

In December 1941, the United States plunged into World War II. Like cities across the nation, Dallas threw itself into the war effort. Dallas factories began to assemble navigation systems and other parts for war planes. When the war was over, these new industries remained. In 1958, Jack Kilby, an engineer at Texas Instruments, invented a radical new means for storing information. It was called the microchip. Kilby's tiny chip helped to trigger the computer revolution that began in the 1960s and 1970s.

By 1963, Dallas was a booming metropolis, its future rich with promise. President John F. Kennedy decided to visit the city on a south-

Jack Kilby poses with his original microchip encased in a glass cover.

Right: Texas governor John Connally, President John F. Kennedy, and First Lady Jacqueline Kennedy riding in the Dallas motorcade shortly before Kennedy and Connally were shot

Below: Lyndon B. Johnson taking the oath of office as president on Air Force One after President Kennedy died

ern tour to launch his campaign for re-election. Kennedy's motorcade cruised past cheering crowds along Dallas's downtown streets. As the presidential limousine passed Dealey Plaza, a shot ripped the air. People screamed in horror. Kennedy slumped forward, blood streaming from a wound in his head. The president was rushed to Dallas's Parkland Hospital, where he was pronounced dead an hour later.

The assassination of President Kennedy shook the nation and the world. For years, this devastating event hung over Dallas like a shroud. For people everywhere, the city's name triggered memories of that fateful day in 1963. Many Dallasites feared that their city was disgraced forever.

From a sixth-floor window of the Texas Schoolbook Depository (below), Lee Harvey Oswald (right) fired the shot that killed President Kennedy.

The Gunman in the Window

Investigation proved that Lee Harvey Oswald, President Kennedy's assassin, fired from a window on the sixth floor of the Texas Schoolbook Depository. Today, the room where Oswald waited for the president's motorcade is the centerpiece of Dallas's Sixth-Floor Museum. The museum focuses on Kennedy's life and legacy and tells the story of the assassination. The window overlooking Dealey Plaza remains ajar, as it was when Oswald fired his deadly shot.

The colorfully lighted buildings of the Dallas nighttime skyline are visible for many miles.

As the years passed, Dallasites worked to put this dark period behind them. They determined to restore Dallas's reputation, to build a city the world would admire once more. In 1967, Dallas voters passed a bond issue to fund massive construction projects in the city. Most spectacular of these projects was the Dallas-Fort Worth Airport, which opened in 1974. The Dallas Arts District was another vast project to enhance the entire Metroplex. Embracing seventeen square blocks in downtown Dallas, the Arts District includes museums, theaters, and even a magnet high school specializing in art and music. The shroud has lifted, and Dallasites again look upon their city with healthy pride.

DALLAS

Each October, more than 3 million people pour into Fair Park east of downtown Dallas. They come to attend the Texas State Fair, the biggest state fair in the country. It is a sixteen-day extravaganza of music, food, fashion shows, rodeos, livestock displays, and daredevil high rides.

The State Fair is an annual highlight of life in Dallas. It is one of the many pleasures and attractions the city has to offer.

A FLURRY OF FESTIVALS

Dallasites love to celebrate bigness. They even boast about their gigantic appetites! If you want to see big eaters in action, drop by the Prairie Dog Chili Cookoff and Pickled Quail-Egg Eating World Championship, held in Dallas each April. No, the chili isn't made from prairie-dog meat. But the pickled eggs really do come from quail, not from chickens. Champion quail-egg eaters compete to see who can gobble the most eggs and break the latest world record.

Competitions of a different kind are held in the nearby town of Grand Prairie at the National Championship Powwow. Native Americans from all over the country gather for contests in traditional Indian dancing. There are also archery contests, foot races, and plenty

A Native American musician at the National Championship Powwow

An Easter gathering in Fair Park

of food. People from dozens of tribes attend. Though their languages and customs differ, the powwow brings everyone together.

If you've ever dreamed of taking to the skies, you won't want to miss the Mesquite Balloon Festival. Dozens of hot-air balloonists assemble to reminisce, compare equipment, and launch their lighter-than-air craft over the Texas plains. Even if you prefer to remain earthbound, it's fun just to watch and take in the excitement.

On the Fourth of July, crowds fill Fair Park for Dallas's annual Freedom Fest. Freedom Fest is an all-day celebration, complete with live bands, quantities of food, and games of chance. The festival culminates with a magnificent fireworks display, the biggest and loudest the city can create.

A young girl with her prize-winning goat at the Texas State Fair

THE SPECTACLE OF SPORTS

Dallasites love sports of all kinds, and the Metroplex hosts five major-league teams. Reunion Arena in downtown Dallas is home to the Dallas Mavericks (basketball) and the Dallas Stars (hockey). The city's soccer team, the Dallas Burn, plays its home games at the Cotton Bowl Stadium in Fair Park.

The Texas Rangers, an American League baseball team, play in the city of Arlington. In 1994, the Rangers moved into a new stadium, remarkable for its unique park within a park. Between two sections of bleachers is an expanse of grass and trees, complete with its own jogging trail.

The Texas Rangers play baseball in Arlington's Ballpark (below).

Texas Ranger baseball player Lee Stevens

Of all Dallas's teams, none lures more spectators than the Dallas Cowboys of the National Football League (NFL). Founded in 1960, the Cowboys vaulted to stardom under the able leadership of stony-faced coach Tom Landry. Fans in the 1990s cheered for running back Emmitt Smith and quarterback Troy Aikman. Over the years, the Cowboys entered seven Super Bowl contests and won championships in four.

Below: A Cowboys-Cardinals football game
Right: A Cowboys football Christmas tree ornament

College football holds a special place in the hearts of Dallas fans. On New Year's Day, Dallasites and TV viewers across the nation watch the annual Cotton Bowl. Played at the stadium in Fair Park, the Cotton Bowl is a contest between two of the country's top college football teams.

This Texas cowboy may compete in roping contests at the many rodeos held in the Dallas area.

Dallasites love to attend rodeos, and they have plenty of opportunities. Mesquite Championship Rodeos are held every Friday and Saturday evening from early April until the end of September. First held in 1958, the Mesquite Championship has grown immensely popular. Season sky-box tickets may sell for as much as $9,000. True devotees are willing to pay the price for the thrill of watching the finest bronco riders and steer ropers in the West.

A glittery rodeo pin

Cowboy hats like this one are worn by many people who attend rodeos.

A lariat like the ones used in rodeo roping contests

ON WITH THE SHOW!

On any given night, the Metroplex offers an overwhelming menu of live performances. The Dallas area hosts some forty community theaters, two opera companies, and thirteen symphony and chamber orchestras. Lovers of the Bard flock to Samuel Grant Park every summer for the Shakespeare Festival of Dallas. Summer crowds also enjoy outdoor musicals in Fair Park. The Dallas Theater Center provides year-round performances of both classic and modern plays.

Opera buffs purchase tickets a year in advance for the Dallas Opera. The opera had its debut in November 1957. It performs in the 3,400-seat Music Hall in Fair Park.

The Dallas Symphony Orchestra holds its concerts at the Morton H. Meyerson Symphony Center in the Dallas Arts District. The Symphony Center building was designed by the famous modern architect I. M. Pei. The Dallas Symphony has thrilled audiences since 1900.

Dallas also has two ballet groups—the Civic Ballet Society and the Metropolitan Ballet.

The Morton H. Meyerson Symphony Center building was designed by I. M. Pei.

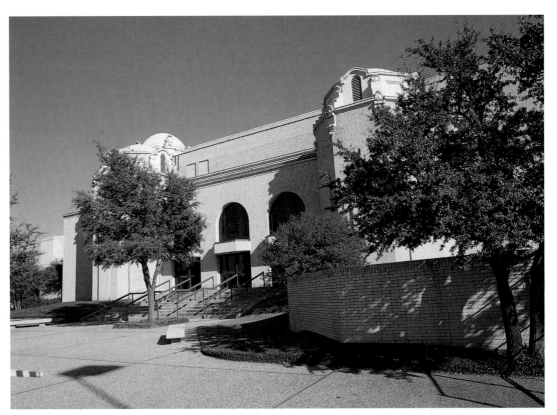

For those who prefer popular fare, Dallas has a wide variety of jazz, rock, and country music performances. During the summer, outdoor concerts draw thousands of people to Metroplex parks. In the world of music, as in so much else, Dallas has something for everyone.

Left: The Music Hall at Fair Park

Below: A young Dallas resident

Strumming the Strings

Each year, some 8,000 musicians and music lovers pour into Dallas for the Greater Southwest Guitar Show. The show features concerts, workshops, and exhibits on guitars and guitar making. This is the biggest show of its kind in the world. Well, after all, it's in Dallas!

BIG D

Many cities have affectionate nicknames. New Yorkers fondly call their home the Big Apple, and Chicagoans say they live in the Windy City. Dallasites sometimes call their city the Big D. The name comes from a 1960s movie called *Big D*, which starred singer/actor Pat Boone. *Big D* was filmed at Fair Park.

The influence of the Big D reaches far beyond the city limits. It extends to Fort Worth, Arlington, and the other cities of the Metroplex. But Dallas has its own unique identity, too. If you want to get to know the Big D, you have to explore from the outer reaches to the heart of downtown.

THE OUTER REACHES

The names Dallas and Fort Worth are often linked together. The two cities are joined by a web of highways, and share the sprawling DFW International Airport. Fort Worth is sometimes referred to as Cow Town because of its long history in the cattle industry. However, that image is changing as Fort Worth acquires more high-tech businesses. The Stockyards National Historic District stands on the northern edge of downtown Fort Worth. Once a maze of stinking slaughterhouses, the district is now a trendy area of shops and restaurants.

One of the most attractive neighborhoods in Fort Worth is Ryan Place. Its stately homes and wide, tree-shaded streets are a legacy of the late nineteenth century. The Log Cabin Village near Trinity Park gives a very different glimpse into the past. The village consists of several restored buildings dating from about 1850. The Van Zandt Cottage was once a supply stop for stagecoaches.

A pewter statue of a longhorn steer

The 1855 J. B. Tomkins cabin in Fort Worth's Log Cabin Village

A fall pond in the beautiful Japanese Garden at the Fort Worth Botanic Garden

Downtown Fort Worth has many unique public facilities. The city's Cultural District includes three art museums and the Fort Worth Museum of Science and History. The Fort Worth Water Gardens are a delightful series of gardens and grassy areas, cooled by fountains and waterfalls.

The Metroplex has made a concerted effort to maintain "green space" where its citizens can enjoy the outdoors. The Dallas area has 337 parks covering some 50,000 acres (20,235 ha) of land. Sixty lakes and reservoirs lie within a 100-mile (161-km) radius of Dallas.

A view of the Fort Worth Water Gardens

Dallasites have rich opportunities to get away from the stress of city life. One of the area's most popular getaway spots is Cedar Hill State Park. The park's 1,826 acres (739 ha) include trails for hiking, biking, and horseback riding. The nearby Joe Pool Reservoir is a welcome retreat on sweltering summer days.

In the early 1980s, the name "Dallas" meant something special to TV viewers. *Dallas* was a wildly popular weekly series, the saga of the super-rich Ewing family of Southfork Ranch. *Dallas* fans still flock to the Dallas Museum in Parker, northeast of the city of Dallas itself. The museum displays photos, costumes, and other memorabilia from the show. Its greatest treasure is the gun that shot JR Ewing in the series' most memorable episode.

A hand-painted saddle magnet from Dallas, Texas

Children grouped around the penguin topiaries at the Dallas Arboretum

LIVING AND LEARNING

The people of Dallas place a high value on education. Forty-four colleges and universities stand within the Metroplex. Southern Methodist University (SMU) in Dallas's University Park is the city's oldest institution of higher learning. Other schools include Dallas Baptist University; the University of Texas at Dallas, with its campus in Richardson; and the University of Dallas, locat-

ed in Irving. The Dallas area is home to many graduate schools for professional training, including the Dallas Theological University Graduate School and Baylor College School of Dentistry. The Metroplex also supports seven two-year community colleges.

Education in Dallas is not confined within the walls of

schools and universities. The city's museums offer a wealth of programs and exhibits to spark the curiosity of people of all ages. Whether your interest is art, science, or history, Dallas's museums will have something special for you.

A building on the SMU campus in Dallas

Left: Artist Mark DiSuvero designed this spectacular sculpture, called Ave, which has a place of honor outside the Dallas Museum of Art.

Below: An exterior view of the Dallas Museum of Art

The Meadows Museum is part of the Owens Fine Arts Center on the campus of Southern Methodist University. A gift from oil tycoon Alger Meadows, the museum focuses on artists from Spain. It contains works by Renaissance masters such as Goya and Velazquez and creations by Picasso and other modern painters.

The Dallas Museum of Art is the crowning glory of the Dallas Arts District. The ultra-modern building houses some 10,000 priceless paintings and sculptures. Works on exhibit range from Inuit ivory carvings to Chinese porcelains, from African beadwork to French watercolors. In 1993, the museum opened a new wing, the Museum of the Americas. This museum covers the history of art in North, Central, and South America, from the pre-Hispanic era through the twentieth century. The Dallas Museum of Art also features an outdoor sculpture garden with large bronze pieces by Rodin, Moore, and others.

Railroad buffs won't want to miss the Age of Steam Railway Museum at Fair Park. Walk through a fully reconstructed train station, vintage 1903, or clamber aboard a passenger train from 1931 and take a seat in the dining car. One of the museum's most prized possessions is a giant locomotive weighing 600 tons (544 metric tons), said to be the largest in the world. Of course. You're in Dallas, don't forget!

Also located in Fair Park is the African American Museum, with extensive exhibits on both African and African-American art and history. Fair Park also contains the Dallas Museum of Natural History, which features the plants and animals of Texas. Near this museum is the Dallas Aquarium, the biggest inland aquarium in the country, with 375 species of fish, reptiles, and amphibians.

The Dallas Aquarium, on the left in this picture, and one of the country's largest Ferris wheels (opposite page), are popular Fair Park destinations.

Families digging for dinosaur bones in Cretaceous Park at the Fort Worth Museum of Science and History

Who Done It?

According to the FBI, Lee Harvey Oswald acted alone when he shot President John F. Kennedy in 1963. But many people believe that Oswald was part of a larger plot to kill the president. The Conspiracy Museum, located not far from the Texas Schoolbook Depository, musters the evidence for conspiracy in the Kennedy assassination. It also explores conspiracy theories about the assassination of Abraham Lincoln, and about assorted plane crashes and other disasters.

Survivors of the Nazi concentration camps of World War II created the Dallas Memorial Center for Holocaust Studies. Exhibits trace the history of Jewish life in Europe from the years before Hitler's rise until liberation after the war. The center includes a research library and a memorial to Holocaust survivors whose families live in the Dallas area.

Early Texas springs to life at the Old City Park Museum. Visitors can explore 37 fully restored buildings dating from 1840 to 1910. The buildings have been brought there from sites around the state. They form a village complete with general store, post office, bank, schoolhouse, train station, and several homes.

A restored Victorian home in Old City Park Museum

A *springtime view of the Dallas Arboretum and Botanical Gardens*

White Rock Lake Park is an oasis for hikers and picnickers on summer days. The Dallas Arboretum and Botanical Gardens stretch along the lake's shores. Paths meander among herb gardens, exotic floral displays, and even vegetable gardens growing squash and rhubarb.

Anyone who loves animals will want to visit the Dallas Zoo in Marsalis Park. About 1,400 birds, mammals, and reptiles are on display, and not all of them are in cages. Riding a monorail train, visitors can see free-roaming gorillas, zebras, antelopes, and other African animals in their re-created natural habitats.

An armadillo magnet

SEEING THE SIGHTS

The landscape of Dallas is dotted with monuments and historic buildings. Each is a landmark beloved to Dallasites and a magnet to visitors. One of Dallas's newest sights is *Texas Longhorn Cattle Drive,* an immense bronze sculpture at the city's Pioneer Plaza. Unveiled in 1994, the sculpture depicts fifty running steers, herded by three cowboys on horseback. The steers charge full tilt down an artificial hill.

Arranged over the 4.2-acre (1.7-ha) plaza, this is the biggest outdoor sculpture on earth.

On Founders Plaza stands a recreation of the log cabin John Neely Bryan built on the Trinity River. Adjoining Founders Plaza is Kennedy Memorial Plaza, with a 30-foot (9-meter) monument to the assassinated president. Each year, thousands of visitors make the pilgrimage to the monument.

From there, they move on to Dealey Plaza, 200 yards (183 m) away. Some snap photos; some leaf through guide books. Many stand in silent homage at the place where Kennedy was struck by Oswald's bullet.

"Old Red" is another familiar Dallas landmark. Built of red sandstone in 1891, this imposing Romanesque structure serves as the courthouse for Dallas County.

The Dallas Farmers Market opened with a cluster of sheds at the beginning of the twentieth century. It expanded during the 1940s and again in 1994. Today, the market sprawls over four city blocks. From March through December, this is the best place in Dallas to buy fresh peaches, strawberries, or watermelons. Even broccoli and spinach from the Farmers Market are a taste treat.

One of the best-known landmarks of Dallas is the white enameled facade of Union Station, once the nerve center of travel in and out of the city. Relatively few travelers reach Dallas by train today. Most zoom to the city on jet planes that swoop to the runways of Dallas-Fort Worth International Airport. Their introduction to Dallas is the bustling, modern DFW complex, where airport and railway station, hotels, office buildings, and even a major sports arena are linked by tunnels and skyways. The planners who designed this astonishing complex were thinking big. Well, what else would you expect? After all, this is Dallas!

This cowboy on horseback is part of the huge Texas Longhorn Cattle Drive *sculpture in Pioneer Plaza.*

These running steers are part of the Texas Longhorn Cattle Drive sculpture in Pioneer Plaza, the largest outdoor sculpture on earth

The Flying Horse

Ever since 1945, the red neon image of a winged horse has floated above the Mobil Oil Building in downtown Dallas. The figure is known as Pegasus, named for the flying horse of Greek mythology. Most Dallasites treasure Pegasus as a symbol of their city. Pegasus was created in honor of the American Petroleum Institute, the first trade convention ever held in Dallas.

FAMOUS LANDMARKS

The Dallas Museum of Natural History

Above: Flowers at the
Dallas Farmers Market

The JFK Memorial
was designed by architect
Philip Johnson.

Dallas Museum of Art
A leading attraction in the
Dallas Arts District, this museum houses more than 10,000
items of sculpture and painting.
The museum covers art from
ancient times to the twentieth
century and represents every
region of the earth. The
Museum of the Americas wing
opened in 1994.

**Age of Steam Railway
Museum**
This museum is one of several
points of interest in Fair Park.
It has an outstanding collection
of vintage railroad cars and
engines, as well as a reconstructed depot from 1903.

**Dallas Museum of Natural
History**
Another Fair Park attraction,
this museum gives special atten-
tion to the plants, animals, and
minerals of Texas. The Hall of
Fossils contains the carefully
reconstructed skeleton of a
mammoth that was unearthed in
the Trinity River.

Dallas Aquarium
Adjacent to the Dallas Museum
of Natural History, the aquarium
has 375 species of fish, reptiles,
and amphibians. It is the largest
inland aquarium in the country.

African American Museum
Also located in Fair Park, this
museum explores African-
American history and art. It
traces African-American culture
back to its roots on the African
continent.

Bible Art Center
Stories from the Bible come to
life in paintings and sculpture at
this unique museum just north
of Dallas. The centerpiece is a
124-foot (38-m) mural, *Miracle
at Pentecost,* by painters Torger
Thompson and Alvin Barnes.

Sixth-Floor Museum
Located on the sixth floor of the
former Texas Schoolbook
Depository, this museum is a
memorial to the life and death
of President John F. Kennedy.
Kennedy's assassination is seen
against the backdrop of life in
the early 1960s.

Kennedy Memorial Plaza
Part of the Dallas County
Historical Plaza, this square has
a memorial to President John F.
Kennedy. Kennedy was actually
shot as he passed Dealey Plaza, a
few hundred yards from the spot
where the memorial now stands.

The Dallas Arboretum and Botanical Gardens in springtime

The Kimbell Art Museum, Fort Worth

The reconstructed John Neely Bryan cabin

Pioneer Plaza

This huge plaza was designed as the setting for a remarkable sculpture, *Texas Longhorn Cattle Drive*. The sculpture depicts fifty running steers herded by three cowboys on horseback.

Old City Park

Thirty-seven buildings from around the state have been relocated to form a reconstructed village. The buildings were originally constructed between 1840 and 1910. The village includes a post office, a bank, a schoolhouse, a dentist's office, and a general store.

Union Station

Opened in 1916, this ornate railway station was once Dallas's hub of transportation. At its peak during World War II, the station saw 250,000 passengers a day. Today, parts of the station have been converted to arcades of shops and restaurants.

Bryan Cabin

John Neely Bryan's log cabin has been reconstructed close to its original site overlooking the Trinity River. From his cabin, Bryan traded with Indians, stagecoach passengers, and buffalo hunters. The cabin stands in the Dallas County Historical Plaza.

Dallas Arboretum and Botanical Gardens

Sixty-six landscaped acres (27 ha) of groves and gardens spread along the shores of Dallas's White Rock Lake. Within the park stands the de Golyer Mansion, a Spanish colonial-style home containing displays of seventeenth- and eighteenth-century European art and furniture.

Dallas Farmers Market

From March through December, hundreds of farmers and flower growers sell their wares at this market, which first opened early in the twentieth century. The market has expanded several times, most recently in 1994.

Dallas Museum

This museum on the Southfork Ranch in Parker, Texas, celebrates the popular TV series *Dallas*. The most popular attraction is the gun that shot series villain JR Ewing in the show's best-remembered episode.

Cultural District, Fort Worth

This downtown district includes the Kimbell Art Museum with European and American works from many periods; the Amon Carter Museum, displaying works by artists of the American West; the Modern Art Museum of Fort Worth; and the Fort Worth Museum of Science and History.

FAST FACTS

POPULATION

City: 1,006,877
Consolidated Metropolitan Area: 4,057,282

AREA

City: 378 square miles
                                               (979 square
                                               kilometers)

Metropolitan Area: 6,491 square miles
                                               (16,812 square
                                               kilometers)

LOCATION   Dallas is located on the plains of north-eastern Texas. The Trinity River, a branch of the Rio Grande, divides the city into two sections, north and south. Dallas is the hub of a metropolitan area known as the Metroplex, which includes Fort Worth, Arlington, Irving, Grand Prairie, Grapevine, Richardson, and many other communities.

CLIMATE   Dallas has a warm, dry climate during most of the year. January temperatures average 46 degrees Fahrenheit (7.8° Celsius), and snowfall is a rare and memorable occurrence. The average July temperature is 85 degrees Fahrenheit (29° C), and the mercury often soars above 100 degrees Fahrenheit (37.7° C). Dallas's rainiest months are April, May, and September.

ECONOMY   Since World War II, Dallas has been heavily involved in the aircraft and defense industries. Dallas factories also make electrical equipment, oil-drilling machinery, processed foods, printed materials, and women's clothing. The Metroplex is home to 100 banks. Dallas has more insurance companies than any other southern city.

CHRONOLOGY

1836
The Republic of Texas breaks away from Mexico.

1841
John Neely Bryan builds a lean-to on the Trinity River, founding the first white settlement at present-day Dallas.

1846–1848
The United States and Mexico fight a war over territory; the peace treaty cedes a large area of land, including Texas, to the United States.

1855
A group of French artists and scientists abandon their settlement of La Reunion and move to Dallas.

1871
Dallas is incorporated as a city.

1872
Dallas becomes a stop on the Houston & Texas Central Railroad.

1907
Herbert Marcus opens the world's first Neiman-Marcus store in Dallas.

1916
Union Station opens.

1936
Dallas hosts the Texas Centennial Exposition.

*A sunny day at
Fair Park in Dallas*

1941–1945
During World War II, Dallas becomes a leader in the aircraft and defense industries.

1958
Jack Kilby of Texas Instruments invents the microchip in Dallas.

1963
President John F. Kennedy is assassinated as his limousine passes Dallas's Dealey Plaza.

1974
Dallas-Fort Worth Airport opens.

1995
Ron Kirk becomes the first African-American mayor in Dallas's history.

1996
Dallas Area Rapid Transit (DART) begins to operate.

DALLAS

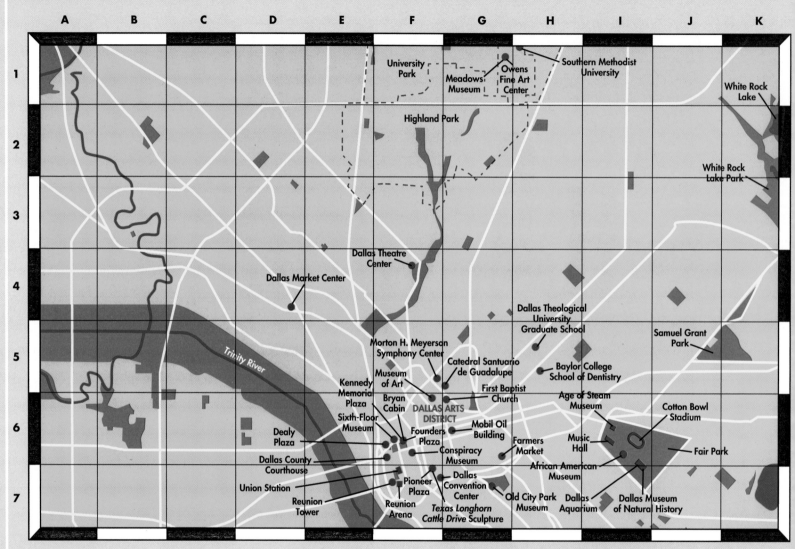

A	**B**	**C**	**D**	**E**	**F**	**G**	**H**	**I**	**J**	**K**

University Park

Meadows Museum

Owens Fine Art Center

Southern Methodist University

White Rock Lake

Highland Park

White Rock Lake Park

Dallas Theatre Center

Dallas Market Center

Dallas Theological University Graduate School

Samuel Grant Park

Trinity River

Morton H. Meyerson Symphony Center

Catedral Santuario de Guadalupe

Baylor College School of Dentistry

Museum of Art

Kennedy Memorial Plaza

Bryan Cabin

First Baptist Church

Age of Steam Museum

Cotton Bowl Stadium

Sixth-Floor Museum

DALLAS ARTS DISTRICT

Founders Plaza

Mobil Oil Building

Music Hall

Dealy Plaza

Farmers Market

Fair Park

Conspiracy Museum

African American Museum

Dallas County Courthouse

Pioneer Plaza

Dallas Convention Center

Old City Park Museum

Dallas Aquarium

Dallas Museum of Natural History

Union Station

Reunion Tower

Reunion Arena

Texas Longhorn Cattle Drive Sculpture

GLOSSARY

aeronautics: Pertaining to aircraft

affluent: Well-to-do, wealthy

ajar: Slightly open

bard: Poet; capitalized, the term is often used in reference to William Shakespeare

cede: To give territory as the result of a treaty

culminate: End spectacularly

debut: First performance

executive: Head of a corporation

facade: Front

Inuit: Eskimo

jurisdiction: Governmental authority

lean-to: Simple shelter with three sides, one side left open to the elements

legacy: Gift bestowed after death

motorcade: Procession of motor vehicles in honor of a celebrity

per capita: Per person

renovate: Renew, remodel

retail: Sold directly to the public

revered: Loved and respected

shroud: Cloth used to wrap a corpse before burial

wholesale: Sold in bulk to stores and businesses

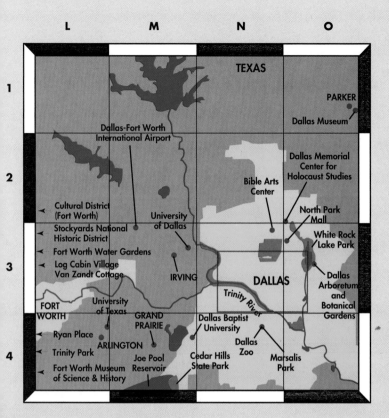

DALLAS & SURROUNDINGS

Picture Identifications

Cover: Dallas skyline viewed from Trinity River green belt; boy wearing cowboy hat; Dallas Cowboys football ornament
Page 1: Cowboy and his horse at the Texas State Fair, Dallas
Pages 4-5: Dallas skyline at sunset
Pages 8-9: Farmers Market, Dallas
Page 9: Dallas cowboy-hat magnet
Pages 18-19: *Emigrants Crossing the Plains*
Pages 32-33: Children on a dragon ride at the Texas State Fair
Page 33: Dallas cow-with-bandana magnet
Pages 42-43: The Dallas Arboretum on the eastern shore of White Rock Lake in White Lake Park

Photo Credits ©:

H. Armstrong Roberts — H. Abernathy, cover (background)
Photo Edit — Mary Steinbacher, cover (front left), 7 (bottom), 11 (top), 38, 39 (bottom right); Spencer Grant, 6; Michael Newman, 10; David Young-Wolff, 13 (bottom), 41 (bottom); Myrleen Cate, 17 (bottom)
Topperscot Inc. — Cover (front right), 37 (top)
Award Design Metals, Inc. — 24 (top)
Dave G. Houser — 7 (top), 16, 52; Jan Butchofsky-Houser, 1, 35 (right); Rankin Harvey, 42-43, 53 (left), 57 (top right)
KK&A, Ltd.: — 3, 9, 14, 15 (top right), 23 (top), 26 (left), 33, 39 (left and top right), 44 (top), 47 (top), 53 (right), 60, 61
Visuals Unlimited — Scott Berner, 4-5, 48; Mark E. Gibson, 46
Stock Options — Lloyd Poissenot, 8-9, 50-51; Jim Zerschling, 17 (top); Marty Perlman, 32-33; Jack Hollingsworth, 34, 35 (left); Dan Hatzenbuehler, 36 (left), 54, 56 (right); J.Z. 90, 40; Andrew Burns, 45, 47 (bottom); ZE8 Schinli, 57 (left)
Liaison Agency — Carolyn A. Herter, 11 (bottom); Edward L. Lallo (MR), 55
UPI/Corbis-Bettmann — 12, 29 (bottom)
Courtesy Neiman-Marcus — 13 (top)
Woodfin Camp & Associates, Inc. — Charlyn Zlotnyk, 15 (top left); Lindsay Hebberd, 51 (right); Bernard Boutrit, 57 (bottom right)
Rainbow — Dan McCoy, 15 (bottom), 31, 49 (top)
North Wind Pictures — 18-19, 20, 23 (bottom), 24 (bottom), 25 (both pictures)
Dallas Historical Society — 21 (both pictures)
Corbis-Bettmann — 22, 26 (right), 29 (top)
Stock Montage, Inc. — 27
AP/Wide World Photos — 28, 30 (top)
SuperStock — 30 (bottom); Eric Carle, 56 (middle); Steve Vidler, 59
Icon SMI — David Selig, 36 (right); Jason Wise, 37 (bottom)
H. Armstrong Roberts — J. Blank, 41, (top), 56 (left)
Log Cabin Village — 44 (bottom)
Unicorn Stock Photos — Martin R. Jones, 49 (bottom)

INDEX

Page numbers in boldface type indicate illustrations

TO FIND OUT MORE

BOOKS

Bumagin, Michael, *Exploring Fort Worth With Children*. Plano, Texas: Republic of Texas Press, 2000.

Donovan, Jim. *Dallas: Shining Star of Texas*. Stillwater, Minn.: Voyager Press, 1994.

Gilbert, John. *Dallas Stars*. Mankato, Minn.: Creative Education, 1996.

Goodman, Michael E. *Dallas Mavericks*. Mankato, Minn.: Creative Education, 1998.

Hampton, Wilborn. *Kennedy Assassinated: The World Mourns*. Cambridge, Mass.: Candlewick Press, 1997.

Italia, Bob. *Football Champions: The Dallas Cowboys*. Edina, Minn.: Abdo & Daughters, 1994.

Oates, Paula and Richard Selcer. *Celebrating 150 Years: The Pictorial History of Fort Worth*. Landmark Publishing, Inc., 1999.

Rafferty, Robert R. and Loys Reynolds. *The Dallas-Fort Worth Metroplex*. Lone Star Guides. Houston: Gulf Publishing Co., 1999.

Threadgill, Kay McCasland. *Exploring Dallas With Children: A Guide for Family Activities*. Plano, Texas: Republic of Texas Press, 1998.

ONLINE SITES

Dallas Museum of Art
http://www.dm-art.org/
A tour of the museum with pictures of current and past exhibitions, visitor information, education programs, libraries, and more

Old City Park
http://www.oldcitypark.org/
This official website of the Dallas County Heritage Society includes a map with links to a virtual tour of all the buildings and activities in the park, with pictures; information on the history of the park and its educational programs; admission and rental information; directions to the site, and more.

Preview Travel Destination Guide: Dallas-Fort Worth
http://dest-previewtravel.aol.com/ DestGuides/0,1208,ACM_64,00.html
A Fodor's Guide that includes links to sights and attractions (with pictures), hotel and restaurant reviews, local maps, visitor information, and much more

The Great State of Texas
http://www.governor.state.tx.us/Texas/ courthouse/Dallas.html
From the office of the governor, this site is probably the best all-round view of the city of Dallas and the state of Texas; includes an inroduction to the state, information on and links to twenty-four Texas cities (with pictures at each site), a map, a history of the state, facts and figures on the economic status of Texas, and much, much more

---

ABOUT THE AUTHOR

Deborah Kent grew up in Little Falls, New Jersey, and received a B.A. in English from Oberlin College. She earned a master's degree from Smith College School for Social Work. After working for four years at the University Settlement House in New York City, she moved to San Miguel de Allende in central Mexico. There she wrote her first young-adult novel, *Belonging*. Ms. Kent is the author of many titles in the Children's Press Cities of the World series. She lives in Chicago with her husband, author R. Conrad Stein, and their daughter, Janna.